Opening up Creativity

Sometimes RE suffers from being the last subject to be planned: every s
often I see children being fed a diet of 'missing word' sheets and pictur
colour or label. But heads, subject leaders and teachers know what goc
quality teaching and learning looks like and that often involves children
learning creatively and teachers teaching creatively.

Many schools where RE is taught well are able to teach RE over several
sessions in a week or fortnight, making it easy for children to remember the
previous learning encountered yesterday rather than having to recall last
week's lesson. These RE weeks or focused learning days allow for inspiring
and creative RE to be taught that is memorable for the children. However,
this book has been planned to support teachers where RE is being taught as
a discrete subject or where meaningful connections are being made to one
or two other areas of the curriculum.

The unit for 4–6 year olds engages their taste buds while embracing some
real RE learning that connects to wider learning on food. The unit on prayer
gives a purpose to the children's work as the learning about Christian prayer
connects directly to the work of Reverend Lynne. Other units use creative
teaching strategies such as a guided visualisation and innovative ways of
encouraging young children to become enquirers into religion and belief.

For the subject leader we have provided a set of pages to support the
planning of RE days and weeks, providing dos and don'ts and some
inspirational ideas and themes to focus on.

Fiona Moss

Editor

Web links: RE Today website

The RE Today website
offers subscribers some
free additional resources
and classroom-ready
materials related to this
publication. Look out for the 'RE
Today on the web' logo at the end
of selected articles.

To access resources:

- go to the RE Today website
  www.retoday.org.uk

- click on the **download login**
  button and use the password
  from this term's issue of *REtoday*
  magazine

- click on **Primary curriculum
  publication – web supplement**

- click on the title of the publication
  and scroll down the page to find
  what you are looking for.

Age focus	Contents	Page
4–6	**Tasty RE: why do people have food at special times?** Fiona Moss	2–6
5–7	**Asking and answering puzzling questions** Stephen Pett	7–12
7–9	**Beautiful messages: teaching sacred text creatively** Rosemary Rivett	13–19
9–11	**Why do Christians pray? Creative learning about prayer** Lat Blaylock	20–26
Subject leader	**How can I plan an RE day or week in my school?** Fiona Moss and Lat Blaylock	27–32
Subject leader	**Using artefacts creatively** Lat Blaylock	33

TASTY RE: WHY DO PEOPLE HAVE FOOD AT SPECIAL TIMES?

For the teacher

Eating is interesting for children and by the time they enter school the concept of a celebration with food and other festivities will be something almost all children have experienced. A birthday cake with candles is an essential part of a birthday celebration and is likely to be a child's earliest introduction to the traditions and customs associated with a special occasion.

Many foods have symbolic meaning and point to a significant story in the history of a religion. As this unit is designed for very young children we have only used examples from Christianity and Judaism. With older children you could explore the offering of food to Hindu deities, giving out of prashad after worship, the Sikh langar, the breaking of the fast (Iftar) in Islam or the symbolism of the different foods at Passover (Pesach).

This unit of work provides the opportunity to explore and encounter the significance of food in religion:

- sharing a celebration meal with others, e.g. holy communion

- special food for special occasions, e.g. why hot cross buns were originally for Easter time

- preparing for the arrival of guests

- offering food to guests

- rituals, e.g. blowing out candles, eating certain foods at certain times.

This unit is designed to form only part of a wider study of food with younger children.

See also

1 General website that will provide information for adults about significant foods, food rules and the reason behind them: www.faithandfood.com

2 BBC Learning Zone Class Clips have several short video clips which focus on the significance of religious food:
  - Shabbat – 3875
  - Leavened and unleavened food – 5953
  - Passover – 3674
  - Prashad – 489

3 Susan Reuben and Sophie Pelham, *Food and Faith*, Frances Lincoln, 2011 (ISBN 9781845079864): a colourful book with photographs designed for 7–11s but the pictures and information could be useful in this unit.

What can children do as a result of this unit?

This article supports children working within the Early Learning goals outlined below, and the pupil-friendly 'I can' statements for level 1 and 2 describe what older or more able pupils may achieve through this work.

Personal, social and emotional development	have a **developing respect** for their own cultures and beliefs and those of other people.
Communication, language and literacy	**use talk** to organise, sequence and clarify thinking, ideas, feelings and events **retell narratives** in the correct sequence, drawing on language patterns of stories
Knowledge and understanding of the world	(i) **investigate** objects and materials by using all their senses . . . look closely at similarities, patterns, difference and change (iii) **ask questions** about why things happen and how things work (v) **begin to know about** their own culture and beliefs and those of other people.
Level 1	I can . . . • **talk about** a type of food: who would eat it and what it means for those people • ***talk about*** *times when I celebrate special times and the importance and meaning that food has in these celebrations.*
Level 2	I can . . . • **retell** the story behind one of the food types in words, drama or pictures • ***create some questions*** *to ask a Jewish or Christian person about why some foods are significant.*

Links across the curriculum

This work is designed to be part of a wider study of food with work across several areas of learning.

The following resources are available for subscribers to download from the RE Today website: www.retoday.org.uk

- Tasty RE judging form for Activity 3
- Set of lotto cards for Activity 5

RE Today
Services

Activity 1   Sharing or scoffing

Ask the children

- Would you prefer to have a small cake, sitting on your own in a room, or go to a room with lots of your friends, choose a small cake and eat it with the group?
- What did most of the class choose? Why?

Share with the children a story of a celebratory occasion you have attended. Describe the interesting food you had, but take care to emphasise the significance of the occasion being celebrated and the people you were sharing it with. It would be useful to share one or two ideas, perhaps a wedding with a cake and birthday meal at your favourite restaurant where the food perhaps has special memories.

Ask the children to

- **describe** a celebration event that they have been to
- **say** what was being celebrated
- **describe** special food that was eaten and why that food was chosen.

Each child can then draw a picture or cut out the shape of some food they remember eating at a celebration. More able children could write a word on the back of the shape or picture to describe either:

- the event, e.g. birthday, Easter, Shabbat
- or their feelings, e.g. excited, tired, happy.

Activity 2   A sharing story

Ask the children whether food is best for sharing or celebrating – which makes people happiest?

Share with the children the beginning of the story 'Starving or sharing'. Stop the story at the end of the third paragraph, at the point where the woman realised that all the people have long chopsticks and forks to use.

Ask the children to make some food or use balls of newspaper to represent food. Invite children to the front of the class to work in a team with mctre-long garden canes to try and eat the 'food'.

- Can anyone get food in their mouth?
- Is there another solution to the problem?

Read the end of the story.

- What do the children think the story teaches us?

 The Taste test chart is available on the REtoday website for subscribers to download and print out: www.retoday.org.uk

Activity 3 Tasty RE

Place a plate in front of each group containing a communion wafer, a hot cross bun, a matzah and – if you have baked it – a slice of challah loaf.

Ask the children to look at each type of food and discuss it in their groups.

- Which of these have you seen before? Where?
- Do you know what any of these are?

Ask each of the children to taste each type of food as you name them and tell them about the symbolism. As they taste the food ask them to put a smiley or sad face to show whether they like the food.

Communion wafer
This is used by Christians during a service at church on a Sunday to remember that Jesus died. It reminds them that he was a real person who lived on earth.

Hot cross bun
A sweet spiced bun with a cross on the top. This bun was originally only available at Easter time. It reminds people that Jesus died on a cross.

Matzah
This is bread without yeast and so it is flat and doesn't rise. It is eaten by Jewish people at Passover when they remember having to leave Egypt so quickly that they couldn't wait for the bread to rise.

Challah loaf
This bread made with eggs and no dairy products reminds Jewish people of the mannah that was given to them from heaven when they were living in the desert with no food.

After trying each of the breads, get the children to form a human bar chart by standing by a picture of the food they liked the best.

Ask the children

- Which food is best for reminding people of what it means? Why?

Taste test	
Food	Draw a smiley face or a sad face
Hot cross bun	
Communion wafer	
Matzah	
Challah loaf	

Starving or sharing

Once upon a time there was a woman who was very old and it was nearly time for her to die. She had led a really good life – helping out when her friends were ill, baking cakes to raise money, shopping for her elderly neighbours, she often put others before herself.

She knew it was her time to die but wanted to know a little about where she might go to when she died. She asked if she could be shown what both heaven and hell look like.

Her request was granted and as she closed her eyes a picture appeared before her. The picture was of an enormous hall. The hall was filled with large round tables, each table was piled high with delicious food and drink. There was succulent fruit, delicious dishes of pasta and cakes of every variety. All around the tables were miserable people, thin and weak. Each of the people held a huge pair of chopsticks or a long spoon or a massively extended fork, but none of them could eat because the utensils that they held were two metres in length.

The woman soon realised that amongst the people there were guards who were preventing people from picking the food up with their hands or in putting the food in their mouths in any way other than with the unusually long utensils. As the woman continued to watch she became aware that no one was able to eat anything, as the utensils were too long to get food into their mouths. Sadly she opened her eyes and the picture of the terrible place faded from view.

She closed her eyes again and at first thought she was seeing the same place. Again she could see an enormous hall, again the hall was filled with large round tables groaning with delicious food and drink, but this time something was different. There were no miserable and thin people here, the air was filled with the sound of chatter and laughter, and the people looked well fed and happy. Yet these people still had two-metre long pairs of chopsticks, or two-metre long spoons or forks. As the woman looked closer she could see why the people were happy – here the people had paired up and were using the long chopsticks, spoons and forks to feed one another. No one was left out; the group worked together to ensure that everyone was fed.

RE Today
Services

Activity 4   Finding out more

As a class, choose one of the foods tasted in Activity 3 to find out more about. Ask the children what they want to find out. What questions have they got about the food chosen?

- Perhaps they want to find out why the Jewish people had to hurry out of Egypt.
- Maybe they are interested to find out when matzah is eaten by Jewish people today.
- They may be interested to see what happens in a church at communion.

If your class has a large community of children from another religion, such as Sikhism, the children may be interested to explore the langar or the giving out of karah prashad during worship.

The children should be given the opportunity to select what to find out more about. It is not necessary to find out more about all of the foods.

You could create:

- a food gallery with drawings of what the children have found out with dictated descriptions or the children's own text beneath them
- a zig-zag book telling the story of one of the foods
- a series of freeze-frames of the children retelling a story of one of the foods.

For suitable resources to support this see page 2.

Activity 5   Lotto

The picture cards on page 5 can be used in several ways to support this learning.

Bingo

Create a bingo card with 4 of the 8 cards. There are lots of combinations you can create. Play bingo by showing the pictures or by describing the meaning of the food or symbol or where it is eaten or naming the item on the card.

Matching

Ask the children to sort the cards into groups. You could specify categories or leave them to make connections and links for themselves. Ask the children to justify why they have chosen to group the cards in this way.

Ask the children to draw another card to add to each of the categories.

Create a parallel set of text cards to match to the pictures, such as the name of the food or the meaning of the food, e.g. reminds Jews of leaving the desert in a hurry.

A set of these is available on the RE Today website for subscribers to download.

Activity 6   Make and share

One of the best ways of remembering something is to get active, so baking one of the foods is a good way to remember the story, significance and symbolism of the food.

Challah recipe

http://tinyurl.com/ckugcd9

Matzah recipe

http://tinyurl.com/c7k79oy

Hot cross bun recipe

http://tinyurl.com/cm3a8af

Share the food with another class. Think about how to prepare the room for sharing food with friends.

- Will the tables be decorated?
- Will everyone have a special place?
- How can you make guests feel welcome?

Activity 7   Role play

Consider how you are going to set up this part of your classroom as part of a wider food exploration.

Is it going to be a kitchen? Will there be some pictorial recipes allowing the children to 'create' the foods discussed in the RE part of the learning? Will there be a table which can be set with candles? Could there be a separate area for dairy and non dairy?

Is it going to be a shop? If so will there be a variety of different foods such as matzah on sale? Allow children to label extra boxes and bags of food that they think customers from different religions or cultures might want.

If you choose to go on to study Sikhism, when finding out more it may be appropriate to set up the role-play area as a Sikh langar.

ASKING AND ANSWERING PUZZLING QUESTIONS

For the teacher

The world is a fascinating, wonderful place, full of puzzles and mysteries – especially if you haven't been in it for long! Children's fascination with life should be encouraged, guarding against the charge that education crushes the questions out of children at school so that they become obsessed instead with the 'right' answers.

RE is a great place for asking questions, because we deal with big questions – and have so many different answers. It is good to help children to see that the biggest questions in life are often the most difficult to answer, that they can take a long time to figure out, and that we may not all agree with the answer when we get it!

This unit gives six creative ideas for encouraging a questioning spirit with children. It gives suggestions to help children:

- raise questions that puzzle them and others
- sort questions into different types, like big and little questions
- respond to questions with some answers of their own, and consider other answers.

These strategies are transferable to other themes, but the focus for these activities will be on **exploring big questions about life, including the natural world.**

This work will link to a wider curriculum study in geography, science, art or literacy on the natural world.

The following resources are available for subscribers to download from the RE Today website: **W**

- a version of page 10 for use on a whiteboard
- a PowerPoint presentation to support this series of activities.

See www.retoday.org.uk

What can children do as a result of this unit?

The following pupil-friendly 'I can' statements describe the learning that may be expected of pupils in the 5–7 age range.

Level   Description of achievement: I can. . .

1
- **talk about** puzzles and mysteries that are interesting, even if we don't know 'the answers'
- *identify* some puzzles and mysteries about our world, our lives and our thoughts
- *experience* the sense of wonder and talk about it.
- *talk about* stories that include mysteries and puzzling questions.

2
- **retell** a story from a religious tradition that asks some puzzling questions
- **identify some answers** that might help Christians or Jewish people make sense of a puzzling question
- *ask some* puzzling **questions** and **talk about** why they are interesting
- *identify* some 'big questions' about life and the world that make people wonder and are difficult to answer.

Tom, age 6, wrote his four questions for God into a poem (see page 9). Could some children in your class do the same? Could an able writer capture the questions for a whole group?

Creative strategies for questioning

Activity 1   Puzzling questions

Place an intriguing object in a fabric bag, or a sealed cardboard box, such as a wooden egg, or an interesting stone/piece of wood, or a plant bulb.

Ask the children

• What do you think I have got in here?

They can guess – some may want to try and see if they can shake the box, weigh it, and so on.

Play 'Twenty Questions' with the children – they can ask questions and you can only answer yes or no.

Talk about what it is like when you don't know something you really want to know.

• How does it feel?

• What will you do to find out the answer?

Reveal what is in the box.

• How do they feel when the mystery is resolved?

• Does the object raise more questions, including those about the world we live in?

• How can they find the answers?

• Which are the best questions?

Tell the children that you will be getting them to ask lots of questions about the world during RE and other subjects this term.

Collect them in a big, colourful, intriguing **'Why?' book**.

Activity 3   Wondering questions – using a story

Giving children a role when listening to a story can help them to ask different kinds of questions – in this case, 'I wonder. . . ?' questions.

Tell the story from the famous Muslim scholar and storyteller, Mullah Nasruddin, 'The walnut and the watermelons' (see page 11).

Get children to close their eyes to use their imagination.

You might stop at different points and ask them:

• what Mullah Nasruddin might be wondering (the story gives some of his wonderings)

• what someone watching him might wonder

• and what they wonder about the story.

Start each question with 'I wonder . . . ?'

Are some of these big questions or little questions?

Activity 2   Big questions, little questions

Two ways of getting children to think about questions:

1 **Ask** the children which is a big question and which is a little question, from the following selection:

   • How much does this chocolate bar cost?/ Why is chocolate nice?

   • When was I born?/ Why was I born?

   • What's for dinner?/ Can we help people who have no food?

   • How many people are there in the world?/ Why do some people have lots and some people have very little?

   • How can we help a sad person?/ What makes me sad?

   A little question might be one with only one right answer, or one where the answer is easy to find out.

   A big question might be one where the answers are complicated, or difficult to agree on, or where no one really knows the answer. These might be something to do with what it means to be human.

2 Have three stations marked A, B and C around the classroom.

   • Show an image of the world from space on the whiteboard.

   • Using the ideas on page 10 as a starting point, put questions A, B and C on the whiteboard.

   • Read the questions and ask children to move to A, B or C, depending on which they think is the bigger question.

   A version of page 10 for use on a whiteboard can be found by subscribers on the RE Today website.

   There is no specific right answer for which of these are the big questions – the 'bigness' of the questions depend on what you are interested in. But the bigger questions are usually hard to answer and may end up with a mystery!

RE Today
Services

Activity 4   Questions for God

If you could ask God four questions, what would you ask?

Tell children that many people believe that God is the only one who can really answer the biggest questions about life.

Tell children that today we want to ask the biggest questions we can think of. One way of thinking up these huge questions is to imagine we can pose them to the person who knows everything: some people say that's God.

Ask the children to

• think/pair/share and come up with the questions they would like to ask God.

A teaching assistant may help children to record the questions, and you might put them onto the whiteboard. Celebrate all of the questions, write them into some cut-out question marks for display, and talk about them.

Show the children Tom's poem (see page 7).

Ask the children

• Do they think he is good at RE?

• Which is his biggest question?

Remind children that Christians, Muslims and Jewish people believe God knows all the answers. Ask them to keep thinking about their big questions. Add all the 'questions for God' to the **'Why?'** book.

Activity 6   Big questions, big answers

Religions offer some answers to big questions raised by life. They don't go all the way and solve all the questions – there is still room for mystery – but many people find the answers helpful.

Ask your children to look at some questions and answers, for example, those provided on page 12.

• Ask the children to match a question to the answers.

There are two answers to each – one might be given by members of the Christian, Jewish or Muslim religions, the other might be given by someone without any particular religious belief. Of course, it is not quite as clear-cut as this. Some 'non-religious' answers may be accepted by some people of faith, too.

Why not invite a visitor from a local faith community and ask them the same questions? See if their answers match any of these.

Activity 5   Chalk, walk and talk

This lesson can be fun if you take the class outside. Walking time is thinking time, so tell them what you plan to do, then go and do it. In advance, chalk a huge question mark onto the school playground, big enough for the whole class to stand around the edge. A masking tape question mark in the school hall is a less exciting but still useful alternative.

Take the **'Why?' book** that the class have been working on.

• Ask the class to stand round the question mark with their toes just on the line. Remind children of all the big questions they have been thinking about.

• Choose one question you know they have enjoyed first, and ask anyone who has got an answer – or even a bit of an answer – to step inside the question mark.

• Hear some of the answers, and praise the children who give them.

• Repeat the process with several questions, encouraging everyone to take some part.

Can the children talk about some of the things they believe and some things which Christians or Muslims believe?

These believers might say:

• God cares for me.
• Each person is special because God made them.
• God loves people.
• The world is a gift from God.
• Life is happier when we love each other.

Talk about why they might say these things.

Activity 3 (part 2) How big are these questions?

Look at the picture of the Earth from space.
Move to A, B or C around the room if you think that question is the BIG question!

A   What shape is that?
B   Who took that picture?
C   What is holding it up?

A   Who made the world?
B   What is the white stuff?
C   Where is England?

A   Where is God?
B   Where is our school?
C   Where is the photographer standing?

A   What is the big blue bit in the middle of
     the picture?
B   Where is this planet?
C   How do people live on this?

© flickriver.com/photos/38152464@N07

A   Why doesn't everyone fall off the bottom?
B   How many people live on this planet?
C   It looks so beautiful from here – is it beautiful up close, too?

A   How big is this planet?
B   Why does the Earth exist?
C   Is there life on other planets?

A   Why is it important to look after the Earth?
B   Is it raining somewhere?
C   How many people on the Earth have enough to eat every day?

A   Are people the most special creatures on the Earth?
B   Why are some parts of the earth warm and some parts cold?
C   Could there be a square planet?

A   If God made this, is he pleased with it?
B   Where is the moon?
C   Who is round the other side?

A   Will this planet always exist?
B   Is the Earth alive?
C   What is on the inside?

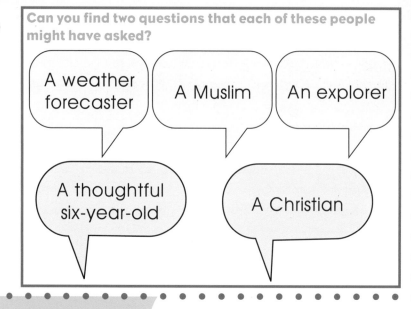

Can you find two questions that each of these people might have asked?

A weather forecaster

A Muslim

An explorer

A thoughtful six-year-old

A Christian

RE Today
Services

The walnut and the watermelons: a Muslim story

One very bright, sunny afternoon, Mullah Nasruddin was sitting in the shade of a walnut tree, admiring the view. The Mullah sat with his back to the broad trunk of the walnut tree, and was pleased how much shade the big tree gave him from the scorching sun. Sitting in the cool of the large shady tree was very relaxing.

Near to the tree, Mullah Nasruddin looked at a field of watermelons growing. The watermelons were large and ripe, with beautiful shiny green stripy skins which gleamed in the sunshine. They looked delicious and thirst-quenching to eat on such a hot day.

As Mullah Nasruddin was resting in the shade, he thought about the tasty watermelons and noticed that they grew lying on the dark soil and grew from very small vines. His mind also wandered to the small walnuts growing on the broad, sturdy tree he was leaning against.

Something puzzled him. He wondered why Allah the creator had made it so that the large, beautiful watermelons grew from such small vines and the tiny walnuts grew from such a majestic, large tree. The Mullah thought to himself that if he had created the world, he would have done things the other way round. He would have made it so that the big tree produced the big, shiny watermelons, and the little vine produced the tiny little brown walnuts.

Just then, a nut dropped off the tree high above his head, and plummeted down through the branches. It landed right on his head with a crack.

As he rubbed his sore head, he looked again at the huge green watermelons growing on the ground. He was so very pleased that Allah, in his wisdom, had created the world in such a way that he had not been hit by one of those huge watermelons crashing down on him and spilling its juicy red flesh all over his head!

I wonder which is easier to eat – watermelon or walnut?

I wonder why Mullah Nasruddin is lazing about under the tree instead of working?

I wonder what kind of amazing God could make such an amazing world as this?

I wonder if everything has a reason?

I wonder if we should be thankful for our world?

I wonder if we should stop and enjoy the view sometimes?

If there is a god, I wonder what God thinks about how we treat the Earth?

I wonder what is the best thing about the world?

I wonder what it is like to be splatted by a watermelon?

RE Today Services

Activity 6 Big questions, big answers

Match the answers to the questions.
Which answers might be given by Christian, Jewish or Muslim people?
Which answers might be given by someone who does not believe in God?

Questions:

Who made the Earth?	What makes people special?	What happens when people die?
Are there angels?	How do we know what is good and bad?	Is there a God?

Answers:

The Earth was created by God. God keeps the whole universe going.	We can work out if something is good or bad by thinking if it hurts people or not.	Angels are messengers from God. Sometimes people see them, but not often.
Angels are just found in made-up stories.	The Earth happened naturally, because of the way the universe works.	God made humans and loves them. That is why people are special.
People are special because they are all different and because people love them.	We can work out what is good or bad, but holy books can help by saying what God thinks.	Yes.
This life is all we have. We live once, so make the most of it.	No.	This life is not the end. Human beings will continue in a new type of life, in heaven, perhaps.

RE Today
Services

Beautiful messages: teaching sacred text creatively

For the teacher

All religions have sacred texts or oral traditions, passed down through generations, which provide the basis for belief and guidance for living.

The activities in this section provide some practical ways through which to engage pupils with the content and impact of such texts on the lives of believers.

Guided visualisation is used as an introductory activity; this is a useful strategy to help pupils engage with some key ideas and concepts found in the texts chosen for study, and also to support them in reflecting on the role of sources of authority and inspiration in their own lives.

The focus is on Islam (the Adhan) and Judaism (the Shema); however, sacred texts from other religions can be used within the structures provided here.

This work could form part of a wider cross-curricular study of messages and meaningful words. It could also form part of a wider study of sacred text in RE. It would also be suitable as part of an RE and Literacy-focused day on messages with meaning.

What can children do as a result of this unit?

The following pupil-friendly 'I can' statements describe the learning that may be expected of pupils in the 7–9 age range.

Level Description of achievement: I can. . .

1
- **identify** in simple terms why sacred texts are important to religious people
- *work out some questions to ask a religious person about the texts they regard as sacred.*

2
- **make a link** between a sacred text and the actions that a believer performs in everyday life
- *ask some questions and suggest some answers about how the teachings of sacred texts influence a believer and what influences me.*

3
- **use the right words** to describe why sacred texts continue to be important to religious people today
- *show that I understand how sacred texts express some beliefs and values for the believer.*

See also

1 **BBC Learning Zone Broadband Clips Library**
A vast searchable database of short clips on many aspects of religions and belief: Prayer in Islam (clips 3056 & 3058); Torah (clips 3666 & 7464); The Shema (clip 3651).
See: www.bbc.co.uk/learningzone/clips

2 *Reflections*
A resource bank of reflective activities, including guided visualisations, for use in RE (ed. Rosemary Rivett, 2nd edn, RE Today, ISBN 978-1-904024-07-1)

3 **The Adhan** (Muslim call to prayer)
YouTube is a good source of sound files.
See: http://bit.ly/ucfOX
See: http://bit.ly/uM77Ay

4 **The Shema** (background information)
See: http://bit.ly/bc5EWe

5 **Mezuzah** (background information)
See: http://bit.ly/vKnjcQ

6 **Tefillin** (background information)
See: http://bit.ly/tlCQFj

Our Children's Children: Celebrating Creativity Competition

This is a competition run by Westhill Endowment in 2011 to provide an opportunity for children to submit their own spiritual and religious thoughts in response to one of three themes: Beautiful Messages; Telling your Story; Questions for God.

Winning entries from the 2011 competition will be posted on the website below, and will provide useful stimulus to your work in RE. Details of any subsequent competitions will also be found here.

See: www.ourchildrenschildren.org.uk

The following resources are available for subscribers to download from the RE Today website

- Pupil response sheets for Activity 2
- Pupil response sheets for Activity 3

W

Activity 1   My beautiful message

Guided visualisation is a useful strategy to help children engage with an idea or concept and support them in reflecting on the role of these in their own lives.

- Explain to pupils that they are being given an opportunity to think deeply and carefully, and then share with the class a 'beautiful message' of their own – an idea or thought they think is meaningful and helpful to others.

- Use the relaxation exercise built into the guided visualisation on page 15, or another one known to you, and then read the script of the visualisation slowly and thoughtfully.

- Give pupils the chance to talk in twos about what thoughts and questions came to their minds, being sensitive to the emotional effect the words 'You are loved' may have on some children.

- Ask pupils to work individually, and to write a beautiful message – some wise and thoughtful words of their own which they hope others will find interesting and helpful. Give them a high-quality piece of paper for their work – something unusually lovely – or use the template on page 16.

- Share the ideas in the class, and consider making them into a class book or displaying them on the school website.

Move on to Activity 2 or 3.

> Some people are like the dark side of the moon and some are like the reflective side. Some people reflect hope and kindness and some argue and fight. So try to reflect the sun's light and be like the gleaming moon.
>
> Jamie

> Be kind to others so we can all live in a happy world. We can do wonderful things. We can run, walk, hold and the list goes on. We can create things and build. We're all wonderful.
>
> Thomas

Activity 2   The Adhan: a beautiful message for Muslims

The Adhan is the Muslim call to prayer. It is called out in Arabic by the muezzin five times a day – inside the mosque, or in Muslim countries from a minaret of the mosque.

- Let pupils hear the Adhan – there are plenty of versions on the internet (see 'See also' box on page 13). Ask them to focus on the sound of the voice, the way the words are pronounced, the pauses between sentences, the 'feel' of it. What sort of sound do they think this is? What might it be used for?

- Show pupils the words of the Adhan in English, using the response sheet on page 17, and explain that for Muslims this is a 'beautiful message'.

- Ask pupils to work together in pairs to respond to the four questions. Play the adhan again while they are working. Feed back their ideas.

- What other 'beautiful messages' might there be for Muslims? Where might they be found? Read with pupils the opening words of Surah 1 of the Qur'an – the Al Fatihah. Why might Muslims find this 'beautiful'?

- Another beautiful message – the message of the Prophet's final sermon is available on page 18.

Activity 3   The Shema: a beautiful message for Jewish people

The Shema is a prayer which makes an important statement about what Jews believe about God. It is found in the Tenakh, the first part of the Jewish Bible.

- Let pupils read the words of the Shema and the statement that follows it (see page 19). What do pupils think Jewish people believe about God? How do we know it's important?

- Show pupils pictures of a variety of mezuzahs and tefillin – an internet image search on 'mezuzah' and 'tefillin' will provide a good selection. Ask pupils to find out more about the sacred text these artefacts contain and how they are used.

- Ask pupils to make a 'mezuzah' for their classroom or for themselves at home – what would it look like, and what would be the 'beautiful message' written inside it? This site will provide the background information to support this task:
  www.beingjewish.com/mitzvos/mezuzah.html

- What other 'beautiful messages' might there be for Jewish people? Where might they be found? Read Genesis chapter 1 in the Bible with pupils – the creation of the world. Why might Jewish people find this 'beautiful'?

- Another beautiful message – a message from the Talmud is available as a response sheet for subscribers to download.

RE Today
Services

My beautiful message: a guided visualisation

Script

I want you to take a few moments to relax, and be still, then join in a guided story with me. You can opt out if you want to, and just sit quietly, but please don't disturb others in the group, who are thinking deeply.

[Pause]

Begin by finding a comfortable position – two feet on the floor, straight back, hands resting in your lap or folded together. Close your eyes, and be still, so that your imagination can work. Spend a bit of time noticing your breathing – you might count your breaths, in and out, for a minute or so. See how calm this can make you.

[Pause]

Now imagine that you are alone, seated in a spacious room. There's a soft evening light outside the open windows, and a warm breeze blowing through them. You feel really relaxed, at home.

[Pause]

The room is quiet – nothing disturbs you. You're not busy – you have plenty of time. There's a big screen TV, so you press the button to start the TV on your remote control. The screen flickers into life. You are pleased to see screenshots of the countryside, seen from above. It's as if you're flying over the countryside, which is lush and green, and it's such a good TV that it feels really realistic. There is rather lovely music, calm and clear. It's almost as if you are there.

[Pause]

The TV programme follows the bird's eye view over countryside, fields and woods, rivers and trees for a minute or two. You enjoy seeing the treetops, the birds, green clearings and mossy glades. Then some text starts to scroll across the bottom of the screen, and you read it.

[Pause]

To your surprise it says, 'the angel is now approaching . . . the angel is now approaching . . . your message from God will be here in a moment . . . your message from God will be here in a moment . . .' You think 'What if an angel brought a message to me?' and the thought is amusing, it makes you curious. But then you think about what such a message would say.

If a message from God, from an angel, came to you, what would it say? You wonder if it would be about your behaviour, your speech, some secret, something you don't want to think of. Across the screen, the words still run: 'your message from God will be here in a moment . . .'

[Pause]

Then you notice that the sweeping scenery on the TV is slowing down, and the flying is coming down, closer to the earth. You recognise your own town, your own area, seen from above. It's like looking at a map, fascinating. The music fades, the TV programme is finished, the screen fades to black and all is quiet.

[Pause]

Then there is a small breath of wind, and something blown gently through the window floats down and falls on to the floor by your chair. It is a rather crumpled pale blue card, with an angel's face printed in gold on it. You feel a bit amazed, and a bit strange, because you are wondering if this card could be your message from an angel, from God. You tell yourself 'don't be silly – it's just rubbish blown in, it's just a TV programme'. But you reach down, pick it up carefully, and turn it over.

There are three words on the card: it says 'You are loved.' You hold it for a moment, trying to decide what to make of it, what to think. The bin is by your chair – you could drop it in. Or you could put it into your pocket. Take a moment to decide what you would do with the card.

[Long pause – up to 45 seconds]

Now we're going to finish our guided story, and come back to being a group in class again. But before you open your eyes, just try to remember exactly how the room looked just before you closed them a few minutes ago – chairs and tables and so on, who was wearing what. Then when you're ready, open your eyes.

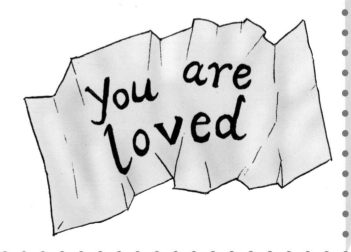

My beautiful message

Some people say that we all have a spiritual message to give to the world, and we all have a job to do in life that no one else can do.

Think: if you could share a message with the whole world, what would your beautiful message be?

Write your beautiful message in the box. You may illustrate it, too, if you wish.

RE Today
Services

A beautiful message for Muslims

1 Why do you think this is a beautiful message for Muslims?

2 What are some of the things Muslims believe that these words express?

© NATRE/David Rose

The Adhan

God is Greatest

I bear witness that there is no god except God

I bear witness that Muhammad is God's messenger

Come to prayer

Come to real salvation

God is Greatest

There is no god except God

1 How do you think Muslim people might *feel* when they have listened to these words?

2 What might they *do* next and why? Write your ideas, and any questions you have.

© NATRE/David Rose

© 2012 RE Today Services
Permission is granted to photocopy this page for use in classroom activities in schools that have purchased this publication.

A beautiful message for Muslims

1 Why do you think this is a beautiful message for Muslims?

2 What are some of the things Muslims believe that these words express?

© Shahida Chowdrey

© 2012 RE Today Services
Permission is granted to photocopy this page for use in classroom activities in schools that have purchased this publication.

Prophet Muhammad's Farewell Sermon (extract)

Hurt no one so that no one may hurt you.

Aid the poor and clothe them as you would clothe yourselves. Remember! One day you will appear before Allah and answer for your deeds.

I leave behind two things, the Qur'an and my example, and if you follow these guides you will not fail.

1 How do you think Muslim people might *feel* when they have listened to these words?

2 What might they *do* next and why? Write your ideas, and any questions you have.

© NATRE/David Rose

A beautiful message for Jewish people

The Shema

Hear, O Israel! The LORD is our God, the Lord alone. You shall love the LORD your God with all your heart and with all your soul and with all your might. Take to heart these instructions with which I charge you this day. Impress them upon your children. Recite them when you stay at home and when you are away, when you lie down and when you get up. Bind them as a sign on your hand and let them serve as a symbol on your forehead; inscribe them on the doorposts of your house and on your gates.

Tanakh: A New Translation of The Holy Scriptures According to the Traditional Hebrew Text (Jewish Publication Society, 1985), Deuteronomy 6:4-8. Used by permission of the publishers.

© iStockphoto.com/ Tova Teitelbaum

© Howard Sandler - Fotolia.com

Activity 3   The Shema – a beautiful message for Jewish people

1 Why do you think that Jewish people think the Shema is a 'beautiful message'?

2 Look carefully at different mezuzot and tefillin. Find out what you can about what they contain and how they are used by some Jewish people in everyday life. Why do you think many Jewish people today still follow the teachings found in the Shema?

3 If you were to make a 'mezuzah' for your classroom or for yourself at home – what would it look like, and what would be the 'beautiful message' written inside it? Explain your choice.

WHY DO CHRISTIANS PRAY?
CREATIVE LEARNING ABOUT PRAYER

For the teacher

In this section of the book, nine Christian prayer cards are used in a sorting, ranking and thinking skills approach to learning about Christian prayer and community life.

The work is designed to enable pupils 9–11 years old to think carefully for themselves about praying and about the beliefs and community living that make sense of Christian practices of prayer. This leads to some opportunities for 'learning from religion' (AT2 work), in which pupils think about their own lives, considering questions of meaning and truth about prayer.

The prayer cards are treated as very simple (and cheap) religious artefacts: real materials made within the religion to nurture faith.

There is an adaptation of the work for younger children aged 6–8 on page 26.

Information file

When learning about Christianity, it is all too easy for the topic of prayer to be learned in formal and rather old-fashioned ways: What does the Lord's Prayer say? What liturgy do Christians use? It is better if the practice of prayer is set in Christian community life, and explored in the light of the learners' own experiences of praying. Note that the practice of prayer is very widespread – maybe ten times more common than church attendance. Lots of people pray, even though they feel agnostic about whether their prayer is answered. Lots of children find prayer a calming or comforting activity. RE should make space for this with sensitivity.

What can children do as a result of this unit?

The following pupil friendly 'I can' statements describe the learning that may be expected of pupils in the 9–11 age range.

Level   Description of achievement: I can. . .

2
- **use religious words** to identify some different times when Christians might pray (e.g. at church, at a christening, in a time of trouble)
- **retell** a story about how a Christian minister helps people during one week
- *ask lots of questions about praying, and look for some answers for myself*
- *respond sensitively to questions about prayer for myself.*

3
- **identify and describe** some Christian beliefs and teachings about prayer
- **describe** how prayer might be used in some different aspects of Christian community life
- list some **similarities and differences** between different occasions when prayer is used
- *make links between my own ideas about praying and Christian practice.*

4
- **use the right words** to show that I **understand** how and why a Christian minister prays for different people
- **apply the idea** of praying as a way of caring for myself
- **enquire into** the reasons why Christian people pray
- *respond thoughtfully to questions about the meaning and purpose of prayer.*

The following resources are available for subscribers to download from the RE Today website: www.retoday.org.uk

A pdf of the prayer cards on pages 22-23.

W

RE Today
Services

Activity 1   Prayer cards and images for meditation

Make a collection of prayer and meditation cards and some 'image cards' from Christianity and other religions. Or create some of your own, or use some made by your pupils. It's a cheap way of gathering 'artefacts' – and leads to lots of learning.

Use the 10 images on pages 22-23 for group and class discussion about spiritual questions – give them to each group in an envelope. These are also available for RE Today subscribers to download: www.retoday. org.uk. Groups of three or four are fine. The story below sets the context for learning and a series of activities for pupils.

On Monday morning, the Christian minister Revd Lynne Coles sits down at her desk and gets out her diary. It says:

Monday	pm: Take the Infants assembly
Tuesday	am: Meet John and Diana about Christening for baby Joe
Wednesday	pm: Meet Evie and Jonathan: Wedding planning
Thursday	1 pm: Mr Stringer's funeral.

She looks in her desk drawer, and finds the nine cards of images and prayers. Which should she take to each of her four appointments? What would she write into each card?

- *Which cards do the pupils think she should take to each of her appointments? Ask them to justify their choices.*

At the primary school, the assembly is great. Then the teacher says 'It's really nice of you to take the Year 6 lesson. We're all looking forward to it, especially because you're doing such a tricky topic: Images of God.' The minister screams inwardly: she has forgotten all about this. But she goes to the lesson, says a quick silent prayer for help and puts the nine cards on the floor in circle time. She asks the pupils: organise these into a Diamond Nine. Which are most to do with God and which are least to do with God? The lesson goes well.

- *Ask your pupils to work in pairs to create this Diamond 9. They will need to discard one of their cards.*

She meets the couple having the baby christened, and does the wedding planning. At the funeral, she gives Mrs Stringer the card she chose for her.

- *Ask pupils: what would you write in these three cards? You could give them some Bible verses to choose from for this part of the task.*

Back at home she checks the diary again.

Friday	Evening: interfaith service. Lead prayers. Muslims, Buddhists, Jews and Christians will be praying together.

She decides to choose three of the nine cards, scan them, and use them as images for prayer and reflection.

- *Ask pupils to choose three images for Revd Lynne and write the prayers she might say at an interfaith celebration, where members of different religions join together to pray.*

We remember Jesus who gave his life for us.
We remember all our happy days and our sad days too.
We remember those who have loved us.
We remember those we have loved.

In our deepest thoughts we find our true selves.
In our deepest friendships we find our chance to love.
In our deepest troubles we find our true light.
In our deepest love we may find God.

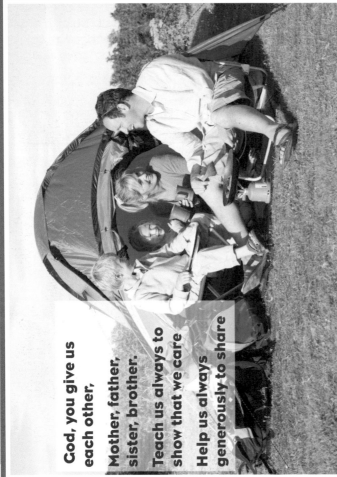

God, you give us
each other,

Mother, father,
sister, brother.

Teach us always to
show that we care

Help us always
generously to share

Thank you God for laughter, fun and play.
Give me the chance today to make other people's lives happy
as well as my own life.
And give me the love to take that chance and spread laughter,
fun and play,
Today and every day.

My Lord God,
give me once more
the courage
to hope.

John Wesley's Rule

Do all the good you can,
By all the means you can,
In all the ways you can,
In all the places you can,
At all the times you can,
To all the people you can,
As long as ever you can.

John Wesley 1703–1791

Violence ends

where love begins.

GOD be in my head
and in my understanding;

GOD be in my eyes,
and in my looking;

GOD be in my mouth,
and in my speaking;

GOD be in my heart,
and in my thinking;

GOD be at my end,
and at my departing.

May our hands
work for justice
and peace

May the God of grace
be helping your
right hand,
now and for ever
till your
resurrection day!

Activity 2   Four letters to Reverend Lynne

The following week, Lynne receives four letters from the people she met. Each one of them asks her to help in some way. Work in a group of four to reply to these letters, as if they are from Reverend Lynne.

Dear Lynne

Thank you so much for coming to our school last week, we liked your lesson about the image of God. In our next RE lesson we are doing: what do Christians believe about God, Jesus and the Holy Spirit?

Please can you tell us what you believe about these three important Christian ideas?

Thank you.

Class 6

Hi Lynne

We're just writing to tell you how thankful we were for your lovely wedding service last week. It was a special day and everything went really well. We haven't been to your church much, but getting married there was lovely, and we are wondering if we might come along more often.

Please tell us what joining the church really means, and how we could get involved.

Thanks

Evie and Jonathan

Dear Lynne

Thanks very much for all your care in planning Baby Joe's welcome to the church last week. It was a great occasion for us, with all the family saying what a lovely service it was. We especially liked the way you made it fun. Now, of course, we have to bring up the lovely little boy to follow Jesus.

Do you have any suggestions for us about how we could do this?

Love

John and Diana

Dear Lynne

Thank you for all your help with the funeral. It was such a comfort to have such a well attended service for my dear husband, and thank you for your kind card, and all your support. Of course I miss him terribly, and have been very sad.

I really don't know how I will go on.

Please keep in touch, and pray for me, in the sad days ahead.

Yours

Betty Stringer

RE Today
Services

Diamond Nine (A)

Arrange the cards in rows of 1-2-3-2-1 with the most child friendly at the top, the least child friendly at the bottom. Do words or images make them child friendly?

Creative stimulus

You work for a card-making company, and they have a brief from a client to devise a new range of spiritual cards that might sell well to people in different religions. What would your designs be like?

Ranking:

If you opened an envelope and found one of these cards in it today sent to you by a person who cares for you, which would you most like to find? Least like to find? Why? Which would you send to the person you care for most? What would you write in it?

Which for whom?

Suggest which of the nine cards you might choose to send to a person getting married, with a new baby, or going to a funeral. Which would you give to an infant school assembly?

Eight things to do with prayer cards and images in RE

Diamond Nine (B)

Which of the nine cards are more to do with God and which are the least to do with God? Use the 1-2-3-2-1 pattern to show your views. (What would an atheist do with this task?)

Prayers for peace between religions

You are writing prayers for the interfaith week of prayer for peace. Which image would you use, and what prayer would you say to go with the image? Can you write three prayers, one for children ages 5–7, one for teenagers, and one to use in a service where people from six religions will be joining together?

Calendar creation

Your group are asked to design three spiritual calendars, with 12 well-chosen and fitting images in each, for each month of the year, one Christian, one Muslim, one Jewish.

Find out lots about the calendars of the different religions – for example, does the Muslim one need 13 months? To save money, the boss wants to use some images the same in each. Choose and justify them.

Interfaith expression

Look at the cards and choose the three which could be related to more than one religion most easily.

Why did you choose these?

Adapting the learning for younger pupils

Although this learning is designed for 9–11 year olds, with a few simple adaptations, some of this material can be accessed by 6–8 year olds who are studying prayer, leaders or a more cross-curricular theme on 'our local community'.

- With 6–8 year olds, you could use the prayer cards in circle time. Make larger sized copies! Lay them out on the floor, looking at each one together as you do.

- Tell the story of Reverend Lynne simply. At each point, ask the children which card she might choose for each occasion, and why. Hear several different views. Suggest what she might write in the card, and talk about alternatives.

- Ask the children why praying for somebody is like a gift. A prayer is generous; some people find it helps them; it is kind, and so on.

- The interfaith prayer activity is too difficult for these pupils: leave it for 9–11 year olds.

- You could extend the story by having her open three 'thank you' emails the following week: from the parents after the baptism, the couple after the wedding and the widow after the funeral. Or you could ask pupils to write these emails – or letters – in role.

- You could ask the children to make a prayer card for themselves, and one to give to someone they care for. Make sure the activity is open, rather than assuming any belief – for example, tell them it can be a reflection or a prayer, addressed to no one in particular or to God.

The following resources are available for subscribers to download from the RE Today website

- The 10 prayer cards from pages 22-23

See: www.retoday.org.uk

RE Today
Services

How can I plan an RE day or week in my school?

For the teacher

Organising the curriculum for high impact

Good Religious Education doesn't need to be bound by rules about 'one lesson a week'. Too often, the subject is given low status by teachers, so pupils don't take it very seriously. Signs of this status problem include being taught mostly or only in PPA time (HLTAs can do a great job there, but teachers should take responsibility), or 'ten in the bed' syndrome, where when the subjects 'roll over', it is always RE that 'falls out'. In some schools which claim to be doing an hour a week of RE, many classes actually do 20 minutes at the end of a long day.

One way of raising the status of the subject is to run RE days that give pupils an intense experience of RE over a short period, or an RE week, where the whole curriculum is organised around an RE theme for a longer period. These kind of events are popular where creative curriculum planning is in place, and both teachers and learners enjoy this kind of approach. In a whole-day experience for pupils, excellent learning can lead to deep thinking, time for creative RE, real opportunities for spiritual development for pupils and new perceptions of RE for all.

Many schools are experimenting with making their curriculum more flexible and running whole-day experiences from groups of pupils on history, drama and the arts, experimental science, sport and even maths. So why not RE? Actually, lots of schools are willing to run an RE day.

Here we give you six starter ideas for topics to think about, and some ready-to-use lesson ideas (adaptable for different topics) on the pages that follow.

The aims of an RE day

Be clear that a day experience like this is for pupils' learning and spiritual development. Plan to focus on the religious educational aims of your work first. Sometimes it is good to have a cross-age focus for the day, a whole-school or key-stage impact in a week – but good RE is only served if aims are clearly RE and clearly met. Step 1 in planning is to set aims for learning about religion and learning from religion in terms that all pupils can achieve.

These four areas might provide a shell for setting your aims:

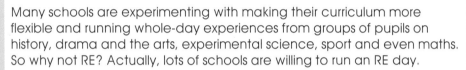

1 Raise and investigate questions about a religious issue or theme (e.g. creation, diversity, worship, good and evil, making our locality better, religious conflict and co-operation)

2 Gather information, consider alternatives and develop thinking on the theme (e.g. by hearing from believers, researching for themselves, doing a survey, working with dilemmas)

> ## On a good RE day, pupils will have opportunities to:

3 Encounter stimulating religious and spiritual materials in compelling ways (e.g. using film and video creatively, using drama, taking part in role play, hearing inspiring talk, tackling group tasks)

4 Make creative, thoughtful and personal responses to the theme (e.g in art, dance, drama, but also reasoned writing, careful thinking, deepening reflection and expression)

Six possible ways of getting into the content of an RE big day

Getting creative with creation

A day of music, drama and arts work that uses the wonder of the natural world, creation stories from Genesis, Hindu tradition or the Qur'an.

- Why do people want to know how the world came into being – what are some of the different ideas?
- Why do religions have narratives that try to explain the beginning of the world?
- Write poetry and create art interpreting the pupils' questions about the world around them.
- Explore the question 'Does a beautiful world mean there must be a wonderful God?'

Big questions

Use methods like 'philosophy for children' to explore big questions with pupils in the morning so that in an afternoon session they can run a really exciting and well-thought-out formal debate that involves everyone.

- Get the children to choose the questions that niggle or interest them:
  o Will I know all the answers when I die?
  o If there is a God, why is there poverty?
- Invite in people from two different religions to express their own ideas about the questions.
- Explore what people do about their beliefs. What do the sacred texts have to say?

Where are all the heroes?

Inspirational leaders – choose your hero

A day to focus on Gandhi, the Prophet Muhammad, Jesus, Martin Luther King, Jackie Pullinger, Mother Teresa or Aung San Suu Kyi or a local religious figure that inspires.

- Ask pupils: 'Who do you most admire and why?'
- Mix discovery, biography, movie clips and dilemmas with young people's own ideas, reactions and views.
- Use a guided visualisation technique to focus on the wisdom shown by inspirational people.
- Each class could take on a different person and create a different outcome: a drama, a film, a poem, a piece of art.
- Share results on the school website, in a gallery or presentation for parents, or in a display at the local library.

Global citizenship

Explore the problems of inequality and poverty, and find out how a charity like Islamic Relief or Christian Aid makes a difference for those whose lives are damaged by war, famine or big business.

- Pupils could do web-based research, or invite visitors to come and share information about the charity.
- They could devise TV ads for the charity, inviting donations and publicising the work. Could they dramatise these, or videotape them?
- Run a role play in which some children take the role of grant applicants to the charity and others are the grant allocations committee.

Easter: did he really?

Set up an experiential set of reflective 'stations' that tell the story of Maundy Thursday, Good Friday and Easter Sunday.

- Explore the experience through story, drama, music, drawing, poems and reflection.
- Get pupils to create their own drama or speaking performances on the human themes of betrayal, loneliness, suffering, despair and hope.
- Ask older children to create a 60-second commercial to be shown at Easter entitled 'Jesus: Why he is/isn't relevant in this decade?'

Why do religions tell stories?

Seek out support from your local library, a storyteller or a theatre group. The whole school could focus on stories from one religion or stories could be used from several religions.

- Explore some of the purpose of stories in religions. Why are they told? How are they told and remembered? Do the stories connect to beliefs?
- Each group could take a story and study it, perhaps finding a way of presenting its meaning in a fresh way for others to understand, using drama, art, animation, dance or some other creative process.
- Alternatively a group of stories with messages could be looked at and groups could write their own story with a message for their school or community, drawing on a message from one of the religious stories studied.

RE Today Services

Plan early

Successful RE days will be planned into the programme for the year, covering areas that cannot be covered elsewhere or that would benefit from a longer period of time to focus on. They need to be planned into the school timetable so nothing else is happening on the same day; they can be 'an event' for which visitors, resources and planning can be organised.

Who will be involved?

Will this be for the whole school including FS1 or will it be a KS2 day? One school that uses this approach has two whole-school days a year and then one just for Year 2 upwards. RE days can also be for just one class or year group. The subject matter will help you decide this.

Visits and visitors

Can you find child-friendly members of faith communities to help with your day? Think about how you will pay them, or show your appreciation if they volunteer. Local Christians, Muslims, Jews or Hindus will be a help. Plan to use them carefully and in child-friendly ways. It can often be time consuming to get visitors and organisations involved, but a day when people can come in and interact with several classes makes this effort more worthwhile. Engaging with authentic voices can show children the diversity of belief, how belief affects people's lives and how belief often leads to action. Engaging in these types of experience is far more memorable for children, making learning deeper. There are organisations and individuals such as speakers from faith communities, charities, poets and theatre companies who are happy to come and work with you – some free and some for a fee. Share what is appropriate for visitors to discuss. The NATRE visitor code of conduct – http://www.natre.org.uk/docstore/rbvs.pdf – is useful for this. A unit on running a multi-faith RE day in your school can be found in a previous book in this series, *Opening up Respect* (RE Today 2011).

Shared planning

The way you approach this depends on the size of your school. Initial plans will probably need to be put together by the co-ordinator and then taken to a planning meeting to decide the specifics of the day for each class. You need to ensure that the day is addressing RE objectives and that there is progression in learning across the age groups. It is a good plan to use the work of some older classes to help the learning of some younger classes – why not have Year 4 work with Year 1, Year 5 with Year 2 and Year 6 with Year 3?

Learning Outside the Classroom (LOTC) – seizing the day!

An RE day is an ideal opportunity for some LOTC, whether this is in the school grounds or beyond. A walking trip to a local faith community building and thoughtful and creative work to follow up can be done on a day like this when it is less disruptive of 'normal lessons'. Also try a creative storytelling approach in the grounds, or setting up some 'stations for reflection' inside the school buildings (there are some good examples on the RE Today members' website).

Advertise RE

Invite school stakeholders such as parents or governors to both support and visit to see what is happening. Can there be 'open school' for the last hour of the day? Could Year 6 pupils make a newspaper in a day which reports all that has been going on, and is distributed free for parents? This may also be a good media opportunity for the school.

Tackling big questions: some starting points for your day

Activity 1   Paper the walls with your wisdom

These learning structures will work with children age 7+ to start children enquiring, investigating and discovering about their own big questions.

- Take 20 prompts such as those in the box on the right, and write each one in the centre of a big piece of flipchart paper.

- Give pupils seven sticky notes each as they begin the RE day, and tell them they will be asking the biggest questions of all today.

- Ask them to choose seven prompts they find interesting and note their numbers on each of the seven notes, then finish the sentences however they want to. Encourage them to be witty – but ask for wisdom and big ideas too.

This approach enables them to set the agenda for an enquiry into the meaning and purpose of life and place of faith. If 30 pupils do seven each, you will get 210 ideas and comments in 15 minutes. If a larger group work on this, then you can get 500+ ideas.

- Ask groups of pupils to take one sheet of the ideas and pick out what is typical, interesting, surprising and fun to report back to the class.

Activity 2   Everybody up! Stay standing if . . .

This is a piece of active theatrical learning which is great for encouraging spoken participation in a big crowd and making everyone feel that they are part of the day.

Ask the whole class or group to stand, then stay standing if they have ever . . .

- seen an animal die (talk about Hindu reverence for all life)

- been surprised by someone taking religion very seriously (talk about commitment and its signs in different faiths)

- changed their mind about a belief (talk about conversion)

- felt that God was near to them (talk about religious experience in different traditions)

- had a premonition that came true (talk about scriptural accounts of visions, dreams of prophecies)

Run round the room with a real or pretend microphone asking questions of those who stay standing. You'll be amazed: they will talk, laugh and think loads. Feed in big religious ideas and questions as you go.

Big questions: 20 prompts for 'paper the walls . . .'

1 I wonder if . . .

2 I'd like to ask God . . .

3 The biggest mystery to me is . . .

4 Humans will always argue about . . .

5 I really disagree with . . .

6 If God is real then . . .

7 If there's no God, then how . . .

8 I believe in . . .

9 I don't believe in . . .

10 When we die, I think . . .

11 After we're dead, I think . . .

12 If I could see the future, I'd look for . . .

13 If I could visit the past, I'd like to . . .

14 We'll never know . . .

15 I am most concerned about . . .

16 Religion is great because . . .

17 Religion causes problems because . . .

18 If Jesus came back, I think he would . . .

19 Why . . .

20 And another thing I'd like to say is . . .

Activity 3   Linking the learning

Begin to discover areas that the children want to discover more about:

- Give every pair in the group one of the 'paper the walls' sheets to review and report back upon, and three huge fill-in question marks.

- Ask them to fill the question marks with what they'd like to have answered about the topics they considered.

The following week or later the same day, start them on a journey into one of their big questions, perhaps by:

- reading and interpreting stories from religions that try to provide answers to the big questions

- emailing or interviewing religious believers about their answers

- reading quotes from sacred text

- creating a piece of art or a poem showing their own response to the big question.

RE Today
Services

Be thought provoking not just entertaining

Think and plan carefully what the children will remember from your day's work, then you have a good chance of enabling good learning, too – but this doesn't happen automatically.

Sometimes at the end of the day the children have been entertained and had fun. But this is not sufficient.

The most important question is

Did the day enable the RE aims to be met?

This intention should lead to some well-structured written work and some purposeful group thinking being built into the day's plans.

Remember that fun + clarity = learning

You must think really carefully about what you say: don't try to communicate the whole doctrine and history of the Christian tradition or a PhD vision of Islam in Britain and the world in your day.

- Don't go over the heads of the children – it's not a theological college.

- Work out what simple points you want pupils to think about and make sure they are communicated from three or four different angles, making the learning engaging.

This is a really important message for any outside speakers you have in on the day as well.

Mix group sizes and ages

For many children it can be refreshing to work in different groupings, perhaps pairing different age classes for part of the day or allowing children an element of choice that will lead to different groupings. Other school ways of organising, such as houses, can be used to create groups for the day.

Always mix small-group work with whole-group sessions and keep them literally on their toes: moving about with kinaesthetic learning is powerful. The examples on the previous page show these kinaesthetic ideas in action.

Create dynamic creative chunks

- Timetable short sessions.

- Try not to speak for more than 10 minutes at a time.

- Interactive tasks will support children in learning together.

- Ensure tasks allow for active rather than passive thinking.

- Judgement tasks are good interactive and thought-provoking activities.

Ask groups to:

- design the new mosque or gurdwara for your town, then plan the opening of the place of worship (how would different faith leaders contribute?)

- devise adverts (papers? TV? radio?) that show what is unique about three different religions

- plan a speech for the candidate for mayor of your town, emphasising how to make peace between communities

- write a collection of prayers and meditations for three different festivals which the class have studied, for young children, older children and grown-ups.

Learning outside the classroom

Use the school grounds as a learning, performing or creative space: space to make a film, a reflection or pilgrimage trail, or a reflective space for the rest of the school.

Allow your youngest children to create a space that is significant to them before exploring the significance of a place of worship to a religious believer.

Visitors can energise learning: a community asset for RE

Invite the local faith communities to send some visitors. They can work alongside pupils, answer questions, share experience and contribute authentic voices.

Often asking a visitor for an assembly or lesson is too brief, and therefore unsatisfactory. An RE day can be a much more useful encounter with people of faith. Include your visitors in your planning wherever possible.

Go in with a bang and go out with a bang

Try and make the day different from the beginning – that could be small scale, such as starting with a whole-school assembly introducing the theme with drama, visitor or video, or arranging the classroom differently. It could be larger scale, with teachers dressed as inspirational characters or walking around the playground protesting at a perceived injustice.

A shared outcome for the day gives children a focus and a reason for you to invite in parents, governors and press. It is important that the whole day is not spent 'polishing' a performance: the day is about having time to engage more deeply with material.

Imaginative and creative learning doesn't fail

It always works to make your day creative. Whether pupils make a collaborative collage of images of heaven, speak a piece of their Divali poetry about light and dark to camera, rewrite a Bible story in twentieth-century rap or dance the body language of the Lord's Prayer, make sure that you give time and space to their creativity. Teachers have planned examples where pupils work together to:

- Take a set of eight photos from a visit to a church or mosque, and put them into PowerPoint. Ask pupils to add captions and both speech and thought bubbles to the people in the pictures, as a way of recounting what they learned from the visit.

- Create a dance routine to go with a piece of religious or spiritual music.

- Make a cardboard model of their perfect street for the future of their town, complete with six different religious buildings.

- Consider what gets crucified in today's world, in the light of learning about the death of Jesus (children suggested in answer to this: celebrities / the environment / anyone who is different / people who are too poor to eat).

- In teams, make a seven-piece collage of the 'days' of creation from Genesis chapter 1, or a 'Then and Now' display about Jewish celebrations at Pesach (Passover), where different groups of children each contribute a 'panel' to a bigger display.

Consider a carousel

A series of activities investigating the same topic for children to engage with. This is particularly useful if you have visitors in for the day. It is important that the children are given the opportunity to reflect on the experiences they have and that there is progression.

RE Today Services